To Jean on Christmas

Love,

Rod Stewart
&

Rod Kuen · ♯

Books By Rod McKuen

POETRY
And Autumn Came
Stanyan Street And Other Sorrows
Listen To The Warm
Lonesome Cities
In Someone's Shadow
Caught In The Quiet
Fields Of Wonder
And To Each Season
Come To Me In Silence
Moment To Moment
Celebrations Of The Heart
Beyond The Boardwalk
Sleep Warm

COLLECTED POEMS
Twelve Years Of Christmas
A Man Alone
With Love . . .
The Carols Of Christmas
Seasons In The Sun
Alone

COLLECTED LYRICS
New Ballads
Pastorale
The Songs Of Rod McKuen
Grand Tour

Beyond The
Boardwalk

Beyond The Boardwalk

Rod McKuen

A CHEVAL BOOK

Distributed by Cheval Books
8440 Santa Monica Boulevard
Los Angeles, California 90069

CONTENTS

INTRODUCTION

The new poems in this collection take a variety of forms and several different meters. Poetry is elastic, but it should be concise . . . a very tight rubber band that won't break when stretched. Not only is it a poet's duty to chronicle his life as he sees it in relationship to the world around him, but more important a poet is a keeper of the language. Not yesterdays or tomorrows, but the language of now. My poetry cannot be judged against those poets who have gone before me or even my contemporaries. I am the poem. The poem is me. No one can safely tell me what my poems should be or should have been, because I lived them. They are my experiences and my feelings and must stand as such. If you read a poem of mine and identify with it, then that poem becomes your experience. You will live it your own way —read into it something I probably never meant to say. That is as it should be.

Auden once told me that my poems were 'letters to the world' and he was 'happy that many of them had come to him and found him out.' If that is so and there are others out there expecting mail, I hope more of my letters go astray.

Finally, a word about critics. If I sell five copies of a book they are unanimous in their praise. If I sell ten, I can expect one dissent. If the number grows to ten thousand my reviewers will always be 'mixed.' At ten million I have detractors of every persuasion, most notably those reviewers who read the statistics not the books. None has a banner bright enough to carry me past the sunset, and no known or unknown legions unsheath swords sharp enough to silence me.

I say again the poem is me. I lived, or am living it. I accept no advice on how it could or should be lived.

The words in this book were started in Oakland, California more than twenty years ago and finished at The Pines in New York in September, 1975. Some of them will be a premiere of sorts for those who think I write only of the lonely and the loner.

Although a poet is neither a seer or a crystal gazer, how can I explain that I wrote the poems in *Campaign Promises* nearly a full year before Watergate? And *A Message To Those Leaving* with its reference to "the Quadraphonic Oval Office" was read by Roy Leonard in Chicago to his radio listeners a full eight months before tapes were publicly known to have existed in the White House, and published in a magazine several months before that. I consider an explanation irrelevant and I don't have one.

The poetry in *To The Last Man Carrying The Last Gun* has had very little re-writing since its inception in 1953. It is an excerpt from a much larger work entitled "Elephant In The Rice Paddy" written about my experiences in Korea and Japan.

The Safari poetry was written on my first trip to Africa in the fall of 1975.

Most of *Love Letters* is very new. *Through The Autumn Field* was recorded as part of the album "Autumn" and *Body Surfing With The Jet Set,* as a part of my "Sea Trilogy."

Southern California seems to contain my most *native* poems (the subject matter and style people associate with me).

Boardwalk II and *Sea Days on the Island* were the last poems written for this book. The latter poem is so new that it does not appear in the first two editions of *Beyond the Boardwalk.*

I say again the poem is me. I lived, or am living it. I accept no advice on how it could or should be lived.

I am grateful for *your* attention and the courtesy you pay me by holding this book in your hands.

ROD McKUEN
The Pines, 1975

To the memory of my mother
and for my brothers
Edward and Bill

This is two books in search of one.

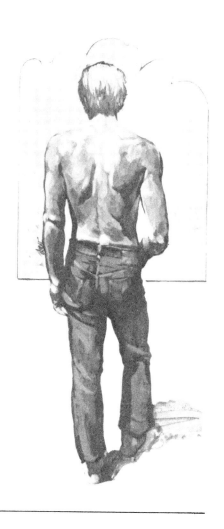

BOARDWALK, I

BRIGHTON, 1

And there you were.
Coming down the boardwalk
       to me
just as though
       we'd planned it
to the last detail,
held a final countdown
to the crucial second.

What should I have done,
run ahead to meet you
stayed until you reached
       your mark?

It wasn't till you passed,
that I made up my mind—
or had my mind
       made up for me,
that I would follow you
up or down boardwalks—
home, to other beaches
       other cities
other worlds.

But I turned too late
you were gone—
       really gone.

I don't know
where you hurried to
if you were on your way
        away from something
or there was some thing
you hurried to.
You were running
even as you walked.
I might have said
            slow down.
I've been there.
I've run too.
There, is always *here.*

One boardwalk's
            like another
and so much time
            is wasted
crawling, cruising,
walking down
        so many boardwalks
in this life and after
that when you finally
learn the lack
of any real mystery
            lurking
on as yet unwalked
        unmarked paths
there may not be
enough time left
to get back home.

BRIGHTON, 2

Today
you came toward me
          once again
as though we'd planned it.
Passing on you smiled
as only beauty
has the charity to do.

Tonight then, in the bar
          I'll know you
by the back of your head
and the front of your smile.

You'll recognize me by my need.

That shouldn't worry you,
remember you looked first.
I'll admit I nearly stumbled
          looking back
but what a sight you were.

Tonight.
Though no plans
have yet been made
I'll be punctual
on time and on my mettle.

I come expecting nothing
(though secretly I know
that there is something
there has to be . . .)
Still whatever happens
is a gift of time
or touch or both.

MIDWAY

For Helen Miljakovich

MIDWAY

The midway
used to lie mid-way
between the muscle beach
                and Venice.

All of us were freaks
in those days
and all of us were friends
Agie, Bob and John and me
and Lenny too
and the Bar was one more
                strutting place
the beach an unfenced zoo.
A different lover every night
made every evening new.

But newness
is knocked down
by the electric crane,
the oncoming bulldozer
the city ordinance
and where people
                are concerned
is trampled, quartered,
scattered to the wind
                by age.

Where awe once lived
foolishness moves in,
then disbelief,
then weariness
            and finally
abandoned and forgotten—
some loves, some awe
however freshly once conceived
become not only old
but out of step
            with anyone
        or anything.

And that's the midway.
From a distance
even rust
and peeling paint
can go unnoticed
or appear as some special
new and kind cosmetic,
but don't look too closely.

The midway
used to lie
       near muscle beach.
There is no mid-way
              any more
everything is left or right,
                yes or no
not even maybe so
              or maybe not.
Stray between the poles
of positive and negative
and you'll be pulled
in one direction
              or the other.

The middle man
        does not exist.
A pity and a joy
for if some wonder
has been lost
in the making up
            of minds,
consolation comes now
from being told
just where we stand
        very early on.

MIRRORS

For Tom Eyen

The side show
has as many sides
as men of midnight
and it shows them all
as finally we learn
all freaks are friendly
for in each of them
we see each other's faces.

The merry-go-round
goes on turning
and every face seems
            just the same
except the smiles on children
fading when their quarters end
        disappearing in the rain.

GALLERY

The target moves
tin elephants
and zebras in a circle.

The marksmen step up
to the dirty counter
pay their fifty cents
            take aim
and one by one
revolving animals
            fall back.

The prize a panda
or a second shot
or even that same
chalked and feathered
        Mae West doll.
And there's the pride
            as yet to come
four column headlines
blazed on the first
            or second page
of hometown papers
for knocking off
        the bully
            down the block
or silencing forever,
            what's-his-name.

THE OLD HOTEL

The old hotel
sits back a block
beyond the boardwalk.
Grey in color,
        once green
                once yellow
and once maroon in trim
if chipped paint
                tells the truth.

There is no walk
and if there was
                a walk before
surely it was made
                from pilings
of twice whitewashed siding
like those that now
                pretend to make
a stairway
        leading
                to a piling porch.

Inside,
framed in fringe
a satin shade
balancing atop
         a narrow pole
is lamp and light enough
and so the lobby's dark
           as Sodom.
Dirty as the hand
        of death,
(seen often on this block)
though never hot
as Dante's Hades—
cool, in fact,
to some engaging.

In one corner
there is movement
or is it one more
set of shadows
playing on the cobwebs
and the other shadows?
No. A paper rustles
or a discontented rat
crawls to another
            corner.

Though I haven't seen
the nile green
            horsehair sofa
sulking at the far end
            of the room
I know it's there
sat upon and spat upon.
            Drooping
like a cardboard medal
on the sagging chest
    of all mankind.

LOVE LETTERS

_____

For Jill Mills

OVAL WINDOW

There is
an oval window
in my bathroom
at Tres Vidas
surrounded by some vines.
Each evening—or almost,
a single geko comes
attracted to the light
there he hangs
against the pane
          till morning.

Being on the inside
I see his underside
beautiful, motionless
                and white.
I wish we had
a meeting language.

I want to know
            about him.
He seems so solitary,
                unafraid.
I'm attracted
to solitary things.

THROUGH THE AUTUMN FIELD

Moths fill up the morning
and spiders slide down shafts
    of sunlight.
The wind now makes a long,
     slow moan.
Tired of all the old Octobers
the moan is more a sigh.
Resigned and lonely
     like those of us
   who face the wind
the wind itself on seeing autumn
     runs to hide.

I walked home
through the field
    alone
looking at the row on row
   of dead cornstalks
frightened by the frost
   arrested by
the first long breath of autumn.
Feeling a little older
but with no new knowledge.

Passing through
        the now past summer
I've learned nothing.

True, I've memorized your thighs
your burnt brown breasts
your eyes, your eyes
but you were busy memorizing
        other people's hands
the kindness
of their summer crotches
the sounding of their sighs.
Without attending
        your same school
as pupil or as teacher
I've become your *familiar*.

                        Bend to me
this first long
                autumn night
or let me bend to you.
Everything and nothing
has passed between us
and tomorrow
            I'll pass by again
through frosted fields
where even pumpkins
now detach themselves
from dead and drying vines.

Autumn is a signpost
                for the leaving.
Whether leading us
to comfort or despair
autumn points the way.

NOVEMBER 17, 1957

Now
as mid November
winds its way
through alleyways
and streets alike,
along the hills
where kites are flying
and bleak trees rattle
with dead and dying leaves,
I find myself in love again
with people hidden in my mind
                    for years.

The loves I knew
on foreign or
familiar shores,
real or imagined,
are all real now.
Can you guess
where my imagination
              takes me
where reality begins
or has its leaving off.
I confess
that sometimes
              I cannot.

SEARCH PARTY

Who is listening
under these calm stars
on this tranquil evening,
who can hear me
and who can know the sounds
my ears are hearing?

We search
because we have to search
because there is no other way.

Because the sky is low
and the world is measured
          in a child's eye
systematically we search
not places or countries
but one another's smiles
              and eyes.
There is no other way
to find ourselves
but in each others faces.

Who is listening
            here and now?
None but the lonely
I would think
for only they
would understand.
Should they lack
            understanding
they'd be the first
to care enough
about themselves
            to learn.

The lonely
are the singers
the ones who have
the loudest voices
when they finally
            open up.

Sing to me
and maybe the music
from your blue guitar
will be the soothing voice
I've wished and waited for.

I have come a long way
wandering down from
silver-red mountains
in search of music
                such as yours,
so sing
and let the music
                once played
satisfy the need I have
to be among the loved
and needed people.

ONCE/A LOSS OF BLOSSOMS

I cannot always say love
            in a garden
and when I do
at times the rose
will turn toward the wall
            and wither.

I wonder then
if I should go on trying
I do/I don't
less and less I do
and more I do not.

My eyes
are just my eyes
but they look longingly
on fields and flower trees
so I suppose in truth
            I cannot stop.
I try/I'll try again.

A loss of blossoms
one, or great wide armfuls
is enough to lose for me
            what liberty
God handed down.

Odin gave an eye
        for wisdom,
gaining yet another
            inner eye.
Why not you?
Why not me.

I will try again
and if I fail
to make the rose
    come forward
I'll seek out
other trees that blossom
and should their flowers
                  fall
before my outer eyes
my inner one
will still remember
  and call back
every flowering birch
     or apple tree
my young heart has known,
my old eyes have seen.
Having once done so
it will not be hard again.

4TH OF JULY

It was the fourth of July
before the balloons went up.
I wasn't sure about your eyes,
but your hands.
            Your hands.

And the calliope kept playing.
And the ferris wheel kept turning.
And the rockets shot high into the sky.

Afterward your hands
resting in your lap
            all the ride home.

TIMEPIECE

For D. O.

My watch still stays
on New South Wales time
and so I'm thirteen hours
up on all my friends.

I wonder
when I come to meet you
if I'll set my clocks
on Pacific Standard Time.

I'm living in the future
till I see you.
The night/the day
        that happens
I doubt that I'll have
        any need
for moving back
into the past.

It's three a.m.
in New South Wales.
If I were there
I'd fondle you
and jostle you awake.

Since I'm not
I watch the clock.
It moves so slowly
that I finally have to
                    turn away.
I'll write a letter
in the morning.
No. I'll start one now, today.

COLORADO SPRINGS

In Colorado Springs
              come Sunday
the bars all close at midnight,
there's no fighting that—
An interloper
         with no instructions
no numbers he can call
is left to his devices.

Larry left a can of beer
         it's almost gone.
Endrigo on the phonograph
has sung his final song.

I've said my prayers
              hurry Tuesday
come quickly, soon.
Fidelity I have,
but there's a half full moon,
coaching me,
         edging me,
thank God no world
exists just now
beyond the confines
of this room.

SEA DAYS ON THE ISLAND

Boardwalks run, turn,
zig-zag, rise and fall
all across the island,
not connected town to town
starting somewhere,
    ending somewhere.

Dependable
        within each village
but never wide or long enough
to span the island
        end to end.

If you would travel
that long island's length,
a surer roadway
        is the sea's edge.

One boardwalk
threading through the Pines
stops abruptly at a thicket
made of gnarled oak
                and pine
            and unnamed vine.

Beyond that boardwalk
lies the meatrack
where no auction
        can be found.
A give-away's in progress
                day or night.

On afternoons
the seekers are at liberty
to choose the right one
first time out.

Not even moonlight
penetrates the trees
when evening comes
as each man
gropes his way to heaven
slowly, stealthily —
silent till he's finally free.

Beyond the meatrack
there's the Grove,
houses clustered like
the meatrack men.

A little friendlier
these citizens
within the grove,
certainly not as circumspect
as all the other villagers
in all the other villages
take care to be.

The Grove displays
the only palace made of ice
that doesn't melt in summer
and yet the skaters
on the dance floor
melt into each other
like proud disappearing puddles.

I haven't gone
beyond the Grove.
My daily trips for mail
between the Pines and Grove
are walk enough.

I've all the shells
and hard round stones
that I might need
and yet I look each day
for starfish dead and dried,
colored glass when Juan
or Eddie walk with me.

Edward's lately taken to Juanito
so I continue on with Juan
or go at sunrise on my own.

Next year I'll travel
to the sunken forest
and maybe farther still
for now I stay content
on my one mile of beach.

Larry's clamming on the bayside.
Laura meets the ferry
and fetches for both of us
the New York Times,
I camp still beside the sea
devoid of any rhymes.

As September starts to shrivel,
and the Island closes up,
I'm content to search the seaside
taking colored glass to Juan,
long thin shells to Larry,
round flat stones for Eddie
and for laughing Laura
love within the plainest shell
that missed the scavenger
and sea scout's eye.

CAMPAIGN PROMISES

For Rebecca Greer

A MESSAGE TO THOSE LEAVING

You outgoing chiefs,
convicted cadre of
elected leaders
found building walls
between free men
        and freedom
not caught red-handed
but hiding out
behind the barn
or beneath the coattails
of the current tenant
of that quadraphonic
        oval office.

You who dared presume
that laws were made
for others not yourselves
and dared to tell us
on the witness stand
that every politician
will perform and has
        performed
the same as you,
I say I disbelieve you.
I say there is honor
        and dishonor
in each profession.
It rests within the man
        and not the job.

I charge you further
with a crime unspeakable.
That of deserting
even for an instant
not your electorate
or your constituent
but the family of man.

I desire not
that you be locked up
or fined some small
              percentage
of the public's money
that you've stolen,
but that you be gone forever.
Away, away with you.
I desire not to have you
in my house.

I am a patriot
and perhaps I wish
that you would disappear
so that I'll not be
reminded and reproached
because my apathy
allowed you, let you
          run amuck.
My own self-centeredness
helped you commit
          your crimes.

My own indecision,
          no decision,
provided you
with hook and ladder
and the dynamite
of disinterest
to carry out your work
while I conveniently
looked other ways.

I am guilty.
Do not serve
my sentence
          for me.
But thank you
for the lesson.

You've provided me
with ample reason
to keep my eyes wide open
          from now on.
You were expensive tutors,
but the republic
      has been saved.
                Be gone.

THINGS DO NOT CHANGE

Things do not change
because of accident or war.
Man isn't altered
(at least not rearranged)
by man himself.

It's not as easy
            as all that.
More complicated
with more complications
man changes
and is changed
      by something else.

Whatever you believe or see,
whatever horoscope you read
whatever bible you consult
God's own ancient diary
or the one you've written
for yourself,
no stars, no sages
and no sayings change us.

What then?
What makes us turn?
I don't know.
I've tried them all
and I don't know.

But I do know
there are accidents
planned
        or perpetrated
that come upon us
like an early fog
and make a difference.

If that fog would last
        or was predictable
then any change
could last
or be controlled.

SOUTHERN CALIFORNIA

For Bruce Bowden

LARGO

For Bill Walsh

Tall men of pride,
raw like November
carry on their shoulders
their weight and more.

You see them not at dockside
but winding up the ferris wheel
or planing beams of light
till they are straight and simple
defused and dull enough
to beautify their plainest lover.

Tall and raw as mid-November.
True men of pride concern themselves
with the worth of smaller things.

KEN

Ken still lifts weights
       in Rome.
Not always bar bells
    but weights.
I envy him
I envy those
who know him well.
Franko, Dewitt Bodeen,
the former Mrs. Eckstine,
       those nightly
on the Roman scene.

He was the freak
I wanted most
     to know
when I was scurrying
      or scrounging
in L.A. a dozen years ago.

I know what made him tick
and land upon his feet
however hard the world
beat and battered him.

Not even T. C. Fox
could keep him down
a formidable opponent
                or an ally
depending on
procurer or producer.

He ticked to tick
he landed on his feet
because most giants do.

Ken,
you might like L.A.
                once again.
Googies isn't Googies anymore,
Dewitt's in London
                last I heard,
and still the expert
with the spoken,
                written word.

But Ken,
new freaks abound
and some of us
who love you still
are still around.

THE STARS ON HOLLYWOOD BLVD.

Vine Street is made
of shredded wheat box tops
held together by the glue
of a hundred promises
that didn't happen
for Whatshisname and Who.

It's what's up front
      that counts.
That made Sir Winston
more than just a cigarette
and John Ireland a star.

FIRE WILL NOT FORGET

You can will the water to be still
the sea to stay as silent
as the unused tomb.
Command the heavens to be cloudless
                and it can be so.
Ask the earth to honor quiet
                   and it will.

Only fire does not forget
nor does it let a man decide
              its movement.
Fire is free.
That makes it able to enslave.
Fire is proud
or why else would it rave
            on hillsides
and rampage through
the city streets.

GENESIS

For Helen Reddy

With zero population tried
and on its way to being proved
it won't be long till all
the mother's milk has dried up
and liberation's had each breast removed.
Not that movements are a cancer,
                understand,
for why should women through the ages
bend and bow to suckle man.

Man's a puny, poor excuse
for what God first
        put here on earth.
Too much tit and self abuse
have made him doubt
        his yet unproven worth.

It will take more movement
on both sides
to bring him back to where he was
if he was ever there
and where was that?
You might ask the question
and expect an answer
        quick and sure.

The truth is
man has only made up
what he didn't understand or know.
At least the female he's been dragging
down the centuries behind him
is finally on her haunches and begins.

With zero population
and the woman finally caring
first about herself
and then for him
man might have a chance again.

BODY SURFING WITH THE JET SET

For Charles De Rohan Chabot

My father's uncle's brother
   married his cousin.
Twice he beat her up
and twice the police came
and twice they carried her away.
Does that make her
       his cousin
twice removed?

       Surf's up.

I keep a loaded pistol
just beneath my bed,
it's nice to have a gun
       that works
in case I lose my head.

       Hang ten.

Perfume makes me sneeze
unless it's tucked up
          underneath
the wings of worker bees.

Beatrice, another friend,
still collects belt buckles.
She leaves her door
unlocked at night
in hopes she might one evening
be accosted by a proper cop
with muscles on his knuckles.

       Wipe Out.

TO THE LAST MAN CARRYING THE LAST GUN

For Anne Swope

TO THE LAST MAN,
CARRYING THE LAST GUN, I
Fort Ord

You, my brother,
don't say you kill
in my name
or in the name
of kind mankind.

If you swing the scythe
or fire the pistol
do so in your own name
mankind has guilt enough
        to shoulder.

You who send the letters
do not issue even once again,
in the name of government
        and justice,
numbered cards to those
        now leaving childhood
asking them to wait in turn
        to fight and die
for those things none of us
have yet been able
        to explain
even to ourselves.

Instead
if there still be
those among you
willing to commit to war,
eager to do battle
for whatever reason
let him who signs the paper
in the poolroom
             or the Pentagon
be the first to shoulder arms
and the only one to feel the bullet
on this side or the other.

No longer must there be
a time for warriors
in the skies
          or on the street.
Too little blood is left
and too much spilled
and no one thing
has yet been proven
that would tell us truly
war is helpful
war is not without
      an element of mercy
war is the convincer,
the credo that as people
we should live by.

The common cause.

War is not the rally
that provides
     a formula for truth.
It is a telescope
whose other end
is always fixed
       on darkness.
The minute man walks
       into war
he starts into a tunnel
       with no end.

Resolve,
promise to yourself,
that if you die for God
you will do so
kneeling with a rifle
propped against your own head
           only.

If you commit yourself
to yourself, your brother
and your country—
     as well you should,
commit yourself to live.
The only battle
that you might perceive
is one where one day
you may be called upon
to war on war.

2

Please tell the boys
you send away
to fight my battles for me
that I have no quarrels
off on foreign shores.

Send them home.

I miss their smiles
              on subways
and their gathering
               on corners
to leer at passing girls.

Conservation oriented
            as I am
I hate to see
tall trees,
especially saplings
cut down and sent off
            to the mill.

No man
is my captain
nor would Whitman
let himself be led
by men of war
if he were living now.

NIGHT GAMES

Soldiers
or would-be soldiers
coming home at night
ragged from the red-hot sun,
dirty from the dust
            they've churned
muddy from the rain.

Half trained
and half believing
in a cause no one explained,
but full exhausted,
too tired even
to make simple dreams.

Soldiers
    out of step
and out of time —
the present
most of them
were given
at their graduation.
A gun. A governmental gift
the government almost always
        fails to stand behind.

SEPTEMBER 28, 1953

Morning now
and memories compete
with one another
for importance.

Where memories are too weak
imagination sneaks in.

I remember,
or do I think I do,
all the lights of home.
Was it last week
or a lifetime of last weeks?

I sit tonight writing poems
one for every dead man
        on a battlefield
and every poem
gets a little shorter
as the list grows longer.

The sergeant thinks me
crazy or a genius
mapping out
a master plan.
Indeed I am
crazy and a genius
like the rest of man.

OCTOBER 3, 1953

That last big moon
rose late last night.
It dawdled on a hillside
resting between two rocks,
crouching before its flight
across the sky.

The stars,
numberless circles of light,
guiding the trucks if need be
as we moved out along the ridge.

Below the hill,
I heard the steady sound of cadence.
Not men but commands of crickets.
And since it was October now
I know this might well be
the last time crickets marched
or made a fuss
before the snow came.

A week has passed
and still no snow,
though every night
is colder now
and every day
a little shorter
than the day before.

Maneuvers still go on
though papers of peace
have passed from general
                    to general
from right side
to wrong side
depending on which side
              you're on.

Twin soldiers
scout the woods ahead,
breaking down the underbrush
and swearing at the rain.
They'd curse the sun's shine
if it did.

I am listening, I am.
Trying hard to understand,
but as the evening
                    takes me in
all I hear is rain.

OCTOBER 8, 1953

My eyes were closed today
to all that happened.

Did I fire a machine gun
sending bullets
down a mountainside?
Did I dig a foxhole
or storm a make-believe ridge
or did I lie back on the green
watching clouds play games?

I cannot remember.

Somewhere in the day
I thought of you
. . . all else was lost.

PRIVATE SPENCER

Private Spencer has a problem
his eyes are lonelier than most.

I saw a woman
follow him half way home once
when that wasn't what he wanted
                              at all.

APRIL 17, 1955

Taegu

While I stood watch
         last night
you walked in sunlight
   another world away.

Afterward,
down the alley
from the P.M.O.
I slept a little warmer
      in closer arms
and smelled the wood smoke
coming from a hundred chimneys.

This morning
it was still dark
the world still real
and black and white.

Driving back
along the KMAG road
I saw Korean soldiers
walking hand in hand.
An old woman
carried a paper umbrella
and a baby on her back.

Near the compound gate
        a girl laughed.
More a chuckling
in the bottom
        of her throat.

All day I waited
for the sun to come.
All day I listened
for the rain to stop.
Now as evening starts
only the lowing of cattle
breaks the monotone of rain.
Only the soba man
        is singing.

LOOKING STRAIGHT AHEAD

I will not let a war or warriors
kill my thirst
        or appetite for love.
Though I do not travel into battle
with roses in the barrel
          of my gun
I still go forward into life
looking straight ahead.

War worries me.
    Not because
the generals lie to us.
I worry
that as each day moves
beneath the cloud of autumn
we may be lying to ourselves
enough to kill what truth existed
when we started out.

I worry that
beneath our helmets
our heads are only capable
            of hating,
that further down
        in our anatomy
we've lost the open space
within each heart set aside
                for love.

I will not let this war
            or any others
kill my appetite for caring.
I'll try to keep some open spaces
beneath and underneath
                my breastplate
        for the next tomorrow.
            Another in my helmet.
There will always be
room for new ideas
to rattle, bounce and jog along.

SUBURB

Tokyo

 The wind moves down the mountain
blowing petals in the temple yard.
A palace long deserted
          decaying like the country
never bothers to look up.

No smoke rises
from those electric chimneys now
where pine wood once sent perfume
floating up above the town.

The Buddha's smile is cracked
but still he smiles.
He's seen the centuries
          of worker ants
bringing progress
              to the countryside
by chopping down the trees
and folding down the hills
to make them flat as California.

WAR IS NOT

War is not
        the murderer,
it is peace.
The waiting for war
the restlessness
men of war have
when there is no fight
no false crusade.

Peace,
it might be argued,
is the killer.
Without contentment
                to fire war
there would be no battle.

A circle.
Peace is not a promise,
only a time
        for reloading.

I do not expect
that this will change
within my lifetime,
or my son's sons.

I do not except
miracles or marvels,
but I know
what war is not
and it is not.

Some wonder in the act of war
still lingers for mankind
after all this time.

And could it be defined,
set down as to its reasons,
perhaps it could be bottled up
or filed away
or even willed away by loving.

But while some men
having tasted so much war
and some who've never
                bitten battle
still walk among us,
there will always be
mysteries to be
    found out.

Does the arrow pierce
and does the cannon sting
and can a private madness
dwelling in one man's head
be stopped by firing over
heads of men he'll never know,
or better still into their hearts.

SAFARI

For Fritz Knoesen

BALLOON OVER AFRICA, 1

For Ray Gallagher

Six A.M.
the chase truck's
        out of fuel.
Never mind
we'll still be in the sky
        by sunrise.

Seven and we're up.
Low hills first
and then green trees
a farmer shouts *come down*
and have a cup of tea
as on we sail.

Now a village
and the natives scatter
we wave and braver now
they shout and signal back
as we slip slowly down
to top the trees.
Hang on
as we go bumping
scraping featherlike
the topmost branches
and you let loose
a Texas rebel yell.

Eight.
The morning sky
is now red diamonds
and as many different shapes
                and sizes
as the sectioned fields.

We'll skim the lake
at left and just ahead. No.
We'll set down in the meadow
just below that far brown knoll.

                Not now.
A little higher first,
a little further yet
surely something lies beyond, beyond,
                        beyond.

Look!
The chase truck's catching up.
Up, up we'll lose it
        and be on our own.
Cattle grazing in a lea look up,
            stand still a moment
                then scatter
over half a dozen acres.

Three white birds below us
pay no attention
as our shadow scrapes them
        like a passing cloud.

Not quite nine.
Two fuel tanks still unused
we can sail straight through
The Valley of a Thousand Hills
and not come down till noon.

The trees we're topping now
        have only tops.
Above
the slightly superstitious sun
plays hide and seek
but warms us anyway
the day is opening
now hills beyond
        the front hills
show themselves
        as we come near.

Cane fields
stretch out
      along the left
on the right side
        chicken farms
          and chicken farms.
A black girl running
        down the road
hides behind
        the sugar stalks
peering at this aberration
                in the sky
confident that she
      can spy on us
        and not be seen.

We let her keep her secrets
and wonder what she'll tell
her unbelieving friends.

> *Hau! Did you see?*
> *Men looking,*
> *but they couldn't find me.*
> *They fly in painted egg*
> *they cook it*
> *light the fire.*

> *Hau! A big egg.*
> *In many colors.*

> *Hau! In the sky!*
> *I threw it with a stone.*
> *Hau! Egg run away.*

A startled springbok
      leaps into the air
and now another and another.
They bound across the valley
           to another hill.

A lake again
and we fire up
to shoot across
      the next big one.

A LION IN THE STREETS OF JO'BURG

For Derek Hannan & Richard Sassoon

There is a lion
in the streets of Jo'Burg.

Head high he slouches
padding down the pavement proud,
untroubled by the traffic
not timid or intimidated
    by the lessor beasts.

Fenced in by the concrete
delicately he threads his way
    along the color line
confused at times
but never condescending.

Proud lion of the street
and city sidewalk
your lair Johannesburg
circled by green hills
even in the wintertime.
Two million
not so sophisticated savages
have helped you hew
from gold dumps
    and flat fields
a city not a town
in only eighty years.

I think sometimes
the tourist and the townships
        ignore or just forget
that this young city
cannot be expected
to be everybody's dream at once.

Perhaps it is enough
that for *some* citizens
dreams do come true.

Perfection
takes a little time
but it is worth the wait.
For one day the lion
in the streets of Jo'Burg
will lie down
with the gentle Springbok.

Even now
he starts to think
    in different ways,
        to wonder,
and that's a start.

BOARDWALK, II

PASSENGERS

For J. S. A.

We are passengers
on the same train.
Destinations far removed
            from one the other
but close enough that you
once entertained the thought
of us arriving and stepping down
at the same stop,
            the self same station
from this vehicle
built for carrying
alike feelings, alike needs.

If the unseen, unknown conductor
            is not known to you,
he is to me.
Beneath his guises and disguises
he is known to me as love.

103

Again I shake my guts out
            not so silently
and boast and brag of love.
If you are so engaged with echoes
it may seemingly come often to me.
I cannot say with certainty
            that it's not so,
but I will not demote, degrade
this aura, this event
      by any lesser name.

I love.
To what degree
this hour and this time
is of no importance.

I love you with what I am
and all I am as of this minute.
Not the hours ahead or yet to come

Friends will say —
and if they do
then they are your friends
                no longer mine —
that I have loved before,
                other places, other times.
And they may even circle
a certain calendar curriculum
and show you without doubt
that they are said to be
                my lovers too.

I say doubt them.
Trust them not.
For I was not invented
                or thought up
until these recent minutes
that heaped atop each other
became these round and recent hours.

In truth
could I not
I would not love you.
I would choose the easy road.
Age has taught me, or I thought it had
how to discover, disguise and avoid
anxiety.

It's not so much that it is difficult
to love and be not loved, or even
that it holds no hope.
It is that the business of so doing
is impractical and incomplete.

At best not being loved affords only
the luxury and latitude of self-pity.

This time
there is some evidence
that knowing you or starting to
has made me better in a known
and in some unknown way.

Ah, but we are greedy men
those of us who come to rest
at last
on what we feel to be
our final, real love.

Better will not do.
We always want the best.
A taste of you has left an ache,
an opening for all the rest.

Passengers we are
traveling these same tracks
carried along by this same ribbon
                    of boardwalk.
All journeys end
or so we are told they should.

The destination looms,
is nearly in our sights.
Can you see it, feel it?

Come closer one more time
and see it through *my* eyes
or stand behind me, hold on tight
and feel it through my shoulders
or feel it while I'm holding you.

There on the beach
beyond the boardwalk
two people stand
            looking into nothing.
Can't you see them?

There behind the snow-fence
        where the track ends
                standing
            staring
some distance from each other.

One is holding little shells
and sea smooth rocks
gathered from some unnamed ocean.
The other's hands are cupped
and filled with chips of colored glass
        retrieved from that same sea.

Side by side they've come
down the same much travelled beach.
And having journeyed for a time
        on the same train
each has loped or run
the distance necessary
to have learned all lessons
        worth the learning.

Now each is gone
beyond the boardwalk separately
            not together
where something surely waits
and found that there was *nothing.*

ABOUT THE AUTHOR

In just over nine years eight of Rod McKuen's books of poetry have sold in excess of eleven million copies in hardcover, making him the best-selling and most widely read poet of our times.

In addition he is the best-selling living author writing in any hardcover medium today. His poetry is taught and studied in schools, colleges, universities and seminaries throughout the world. In 1975 he was the first major artist who insisted on performing concerts before multiracial audiences in South Africa, and was allowed by the government to do so.

Mr. McKuen is the composer of more than fifteen hundred songs that have been translated into Spanish, French, Dutch, German, Russian, Japanese, Czechoslovakian, Chinese, Norwegian, Afrikaans and Italian, among other languages. They account for the sale of more than one hundred eighty million records. His songs include: *Jean, Love's Been Good To Me, The Importance Of The Rose, Ally Ally, Oxen Free,* and several dozen songs with French composer Jacques Brel, including: *If You Go Away, Come Jef, Port Of Amsterdam,* and *Seasons In The Sun.* Both writers term their writing habits together as three distinct methods; collaboration, adaptation and translation.

Mr. McKuen's film music has twice been nominated for Motion Picture Academy Awards ("The Prime Of Miss Jean Brodie" and "A Boy Named Charlie Brown"). His classical music, including symphonies, concertos, piano sonatas and his very popular *Adagio For Harp & Strings,* is performed by leading orchestras. In May 1972, London's

Royal Philharmonic premiered his *Concerto No. 3 For Piano & Orchestra,* and a suite, *The Plains Of My Country.* In 1973, the Louisville Orchestra commissioned Mr. McKuen to compose a suite for orchestra and narrator, entitled *The City.* It was premiered in Louisville and Danville, Kentucky in October 1973, and was subsequently nominated for a Pulitzer Prize in Music.

His *Symphony No. 3,* commissioned by the Menninger Foundation in honor of their fiftieth anniversary, was premiered in 1975 in Topeka, Kansas.

Before becoming a best-selling author and composer, Mr. McKuen worked as a laborer, radio disc jockey and newspaper columnist. He spent two years in the Army, during and after the Korean War.

Rod McKuen makes his home in California in a rambling Spanish house, which he shares with a menagerie of old English sheep dogs and a dozen cats. He likes outdoor sports and driving, and has recently started taking flying lessons.

As a balloonist he has flown with his pilot, Ray Gallagher, in the skies above the western United States and South Africa.

At present he is working on a musical production for Broadway and has just completed the libretto and music for a rock opera, "The Black Eagle" and a new book of prose & poetry "Under the Southern Sun."

Much of the author's time is now spent working for and with his non-profit foundation Animal Concern.